TO FAITHFUL BELIEVERS,
WHO STAND TALL
AMID THE PRESSURES
AND TEMPTATIONS OF LIFE.

Table of Contents

You Can Stand Tall Introduction by Dr. James Scudder   **9**

Your W-D Degree Foreword by Julie Dearyan   **13**

1. A Foundation of Character Why Character is Crucial   **15**

2. The Lure of Temptation And How to Resist It   **23**

3. The Price of a Pawn Defying Peer Pressure   **35**

4. If It Feels Good Don't Do It!   **45**

5. Standing Watch Practical Principles for Protecting Your Purity   **53**

You Can Stand Tall!

*Alike for the nation and the individual,
the one indispensable requisite is character.*
Theodore Roosevelt

In the decade of the nineties, we were told that character as a virtue wasn't really all that important. In the public school system, our children were taught that there is no right and wrong, that there is no absolute truth, and that morals were relative. The thinking was, what you believe is right, is right. What I believe is right, is also right.

We had a president who told the nation that character doesn't matter. All that matters is how much money we have in our pocketbook.

Then, on September 11th, 2001, America was attacked. Suddenly, people began to realize what was truly important. They stopped worrying about their portfolios and wondered if their families were inside the World Trade Center or the Pentagon. People put aside their self-interest and helped in the rescue effort, whether it was firemen and policemen in New York City or thousands of people around the country who donated time, blood, and money for the effort. We also began realizing how important it was to be patriotic and to support the United States.

It was the day that America rediscovered character. Suddenly, there was good and evil. There really was right and wrong. There really were moral absolutes and a God in control of the universe.

At that time in our nation, we once again looked to men and

women who possessed character and integrity, like our President and the other leaders in Washington. We hailed as heroes, not athletes or entertainers, but firemen and policemen who put their lives on the line.

In the 1990's, character may not have been important, but in the twenty-first century, we're embracing it once again.

CHRISTIANS WITH CHARACTER

Though we live in a world that urges us to compromise, it is Christians who should be the standard-bearers of character in society. Often, this may mean sacrifice. The Christian business-owner may see his profits cut short because he refuses to engage in questionable practices. A college student may face scorn because he rejects the party atmosphere on campus. A pastor may see his attendance dip because he speaks the truth of Scripture.

To stand tall in your community, your church, and in your family, it takes sacrifice and commitment. There may not be much glory. There may not be much praise. Yet, the rewards of integrity are not measured in the short term. They are seen down the road.

In this book, Standing Tall, we'll examine the lives of three individuals in Scripture. Joseph had an unfortunate childhood, a poor example at home, unjust behavior in the workplace, and a friend who let him down. Still, these circumstances didn't cut short his character. We'll see how he persevered through hardship to become a leader in Egypt.

We'll also look at the little-known daughter of Herodias, who faced a similar test of character. She too was born into a dysfunctional family and had poor examples at home. Unfortunately, she allowed herself to be pawned into making poor life decisions. From her story, we'll glean important lessons on self-respect, peer pressure, and courage.

Lastly, we'll look at Samson, a man who could have been a great leader in Israel, but instead chose the path of self-indulgence. Especially gifted by God, Samson had many opportunities to make the right choice, but instead fulfilled the desires of his flesh. From his story we'll see the marvelous story of God's grace and how he can use a man even as flawed as Samson to perform great acts of service.

How You Can Stand Tall

Most people think integrity is something that only the spiritual giants can achieve, but this is not true. God has given every Christian the power to live right through His Holy Spirit. This is great news for you and me. We can stand tall in a world of compromise, if we follow God's prescription for character.

You can begin now to live a life of integrity. You can stand tall in your home, in your community, and in your world.

James A. Scudder

Dr. James A. Scudder
February, 2002

Your W-D Degree

Sow a thought, reap an act; sow an act, reap a habit; sow a habit, reap a character; sow a character, reap a destiny.
Traditional

I remember that morning like it was yesterday. I was eight years old, tying my shoes in the living room, listening to the radio. The preacher preached his heart out, despite the hour. Dad and Mom were eating breakfast.

"I want my W.D. Degree!" the preacher exclaimed. "My Well Done Degree-that's the only degree that matters! I want my Lord to say, "Well done thou good and faithful servant."

"Amen!" Dad echoed. And I knew, even at eight, that getting his W.D. Degree was my Dad's heart cry as well. It had always been his greatest desire and today, everyone who knows him, knows that this is still his rallying call. As I've observed him throughout the years, it is his willing heart that stands out the most. He cares about others--he cares not for himself. His giving spirit is something that goes beyond what most people are willing to give, and I think one of the primary reasons for this is his strong character. He knows that integrity is one of the most important aspects of the Christian life, and you will find in this book helpful advice from someone who has made a quest for character a fundamental element of his life.

There are many people who desire to show evidence of strong character, yet it sometimes seems that there aren't as many who understand that character is found in everyday life. 24/7 faithfulness to ministry, loyalty to one's spouse, dedication to purity, a day-by-day relationship with the Almighty, those moments when you want to rail at the person who cut in front of you in the grocery store line, but then realize that he or she is in need of God's love, those times define true character. When you read this book, you will be inspired to continue your character quest. You will realize that having good character is not only achievable, but God has already given you the tools you need to reach it.

In Second Corinthians 1:12, Paul says, "For our rejoicing is this, the testimony of our conscience, that in simplicity and godly sincerity, not with fleshly wisdom, but by the grace of God, we have had our conversation in the world, and more abundantly to you-ward." The word "conversation" from the Greek word, anastrepho, which means "to busy yourself", "to live," extends past our speech. It touches every aspect of life. How Paul lived his life was important to him. He knew that there was only one way to successfully live the Christian life--in the over-shadowing power of the Holy Spirit.

Enjoy this book, It will bring you encouragement as you pursue your own W.D. Degree!

Julie Scudder Dearyan
Senior Editor
Partners Magazine

- ONE -

A Foundation of Character

When building the Sears Tower, North America's tallest building, contractors had to begin with a foundation that went down 110 feet below the ground and into the solid rock layer of the earth called bedrock. The foundation consisted of huge steel structures encased in 2 million cubic feet of concrete, enough concrete to build a five-mile stretch of an eight-lane highway.

The architects of the Sears Tower designed such an elaborate base so that the skyscraper would stand when the wind and rain beat against it. The foundation also had to be strong so that the weight of the gigantic building would not cause it to collapse.

Character is the foundation upon which a Christian's witness is built. If we are to be lights in the world, we must be men and women of integrity. When the winds of skepticism beat against us, strong character will keep onlookers from doubting the reality of our faith.

Usually, it is the lifestyle and behavior of Christians in their midst that has the most influence upon the mind of nonbelievers. Seekers who discover hypocrisy, open sin, or a disregard for the Word of God in Christians find cause to reject the Gospel.

To ensure a durable footing, the foundation of character is made up several attributes. This is not an exhaustive list, but perhaps the five most important pillars of a man or woman of integrity.

Honesty is the Best Policy

Dr. Madison Saratt, a mathematics teacher at Vanderbilt University for many years, offered one piece of advice before handing out a test. He would say something like this, "Today, I am giving you two examinations, one in trigonometry and the other in honesty. There are many good people in the world who cannot pass trigonometry, but there are no good people who cannot pass the examination of honesty."

Honesty may be the most important ingredient of character, yet the least respected. We find no problem keeping the extra change at the checkout. We don't think twice about lying about our kids' age at the buffet. And there is no problem with fudging the hours on our timecard.

The Apostle Paul said that a committed Christian will seek out honesty in all his dealings: "Providing for honest things, not only in the sight of the Lord, but also in the sight of men." (2 Corinthians 8:21)

It is impossible to live without telling a lie. We are sinners by nature and lying is one of those sometimes overlooked sins. However, there is a difference between someone who makes a conscience effort to tell the truth and another who lies habitually to benefit himself.

According to the Apostle Peter, the world notices an honest man: "Having your conversation honest among the Gentiles: that, whereas they speak against you as evildoers, they may by your good works, which they shall behold, glorify God in the day of visitation." (1 Peter 2:12)

Keeping your word may be the difference between an unsaved person accepting Christ and rejecting Him. It may be a coworker you have never met. It may be a relative in a distant state. It may be a creditor who has never seen your face. It may be your only chance of winning him to the Lord. You will probably never know that you are being watched.

Make a commitment to honesty, even if it costs you something. This oft-neglected virtue is sure-fire signal of your faith to the observing world.

It's Not About You

The climate is unbearably hot. The sanitation is terrible. The long plane flight is weary. These and other conditions make the annual missions trip to India anything but a vacation. Yet, God has led me to this great land because there is a tremendous harvest of souls. The bright smiles adorn the faces of young and old who come to Christ as a result of the gospel preaching.

Serving God includes giving of ourselves, even when it's tough. God may call us to circumstances that are different than we are accustomed to. Yet, if we desire to accomplish great things for Him, we must sacrifice our personal desires.

We take our example from the most selfless Person who ever lived, Jesus Christ. He gave up a home in Heaven to enter this sinful world. He died a cruel physical death and bore the sin and guilt of the entire human race. Had He had His own interests at heart, He would have never died for us.

In our padded culture, we are used to getting what we want when we want it. We're used to calling our own shots and having things our way. Yet, Christ calls us to a different lifestyle.

"But he that is greatest among you shall be your servant. And whosoever shall exalt himself shall be abased; and he that shall humble himself shall be exalted." (Matthew 23:11-12)

Selflessness is the catalyst of your character. Build this important trait into your life. Determine to put yourself last. By minimizing yourself, you'll become great in God's family.

Action Tells the Story

Perhaps the world's greatest athlete, Michael Jordan, did things with the basketball that still leave fans shaking their heads. He was able to leap high over defenders, twist his body and drop the ball into the basket with ease. For over a decade, he led the league in scoring and led the Chicago Bulls to six championships.

Even though Jordan was talented, it was not his physical abilities that made him great. It was his approach to the game of basketball. Few people understand the depth of commitment he had. The day after each championship victory, Michael Jordan began preparing for the next season. Every morning, he rose early and began a grueling workout, lifting weights, running, and working on his shot. There were other guys with similar talent, who after a few years in the league became mediocre. The secret to Jordan's greatness was his devotion to the game.

The secret to the Christian life is commitment. I look at the level of dedication Michael Jordan had to basketball, a meaningless game, and wonder what would happen if Christians had that same dedication to the cause of Christ. The world wouldn't be the same. Romans declares this to be our reasonable service:

"I beseech you therefore, brethren, by the mercies of God, that ye present your bodies a living sacrifice, holy, acceptable unto God, which is your reasonable service." (Romans 12:1)

Christian character begins and ends with commitment. Scores of people have told me how much they care about the Lord, how deep their love is, and how concerned they are for the lost. Yet, not as many have backed up their lofty words with actions. Words are touching, but action tells the story.

Here are a few areas of your life where your commitment is most important:

Personal Devotions

Commit to a regular pattern of Bible reading and prayer. Find a time and a place where you can get alone and meditate. Then, make it a regular habit to visit that place every day, even when you don't feel like it. (Joshua 1:8)

Church Attendance every time the doors are open. Volunteer for projects and ministries where you can be useful, even if it involves something you don't particularly enjoy doing. (Hebrews 10:25)

Marriage Strive to be the husband or wife that God intends you to be. Listen to your mate. Read, listen, and learn all you can about becoming a godly spouse. Solve marital conflicts early. Make time for your husband or wife. (Ephesians 5:22-26)

Children Ignore what the world has to say about raising children. Dig deep into God's Word and make a commitment to biblical child-training. Make time for your children. Bring them to church, pray with them, and encourage them to get close to God. (Proverbs 22:6; Deuteronomy 6:7)

Vocation Be a reliable, trustworthy employee. Work hard from 9 to 5. Be obedient to your superiors. Don't backstab your bosses. Be an example to the other employees, even if it makes you a little different. (Proverbs 25:13: Ephesians 6:6; Titus 2:9)

PLEDGING ALLEGIANCE

There is a movement afoot in Christianity that says unity in a church is wrong. Many books have been written and numerous seminars have been conducted, instructing believers how to question the authority in a church and initiate conflict. They seem to think that the church is a sort of democracy where everybody gets a vote and everybody speaks their mind.

I'm not at all for a dictatorial style of leadership in the church or in the home, but I do believe that the New Testament preaches loyalty to the body of Christ. Consider the Apostle Paul's words to the church at Philippi:

"If there be therefore any consolation in Christ, if any comfort of love, if any fellowship of the Spirit, if any bowels and mercies, Fulfil ye my joy, that ye be likeminded, having the same love, being of one accord, of one mind." (Philippians 2:1-2)

Even though loyalty is a lost art today, it should be characteristic of the Christian. Our first loyalty should be to Christ, but many times we use that as an excuse to be disloyal to our brothers and sisters in Christ. Loyalty to Christ, however, will never be cause for disloyalty to a good, Bible-believing church, to our families, and to our employer.

Now, our loyalties can be misplaced. God doesn't expect us to follow false teachers and movements that harm our faith. Loyalty shouldn't extend to compromising our standards.

The line is drawn when our allegiance forces us to sin against God. People who work in the secular field understand this. If the boss asks you to drink or engage in immoral practices, then you can claim loyalty to Christ. If a church begins embracing false doctrines, then your loyalty is to Christ.

Most of the time, however, we are disloyal because it suits our interests. A spouse doesn't feel the same "love" that was present early in the marriage, so he opts for divorce. An employee doesn't like his boss's personality, so he jumps ship to another company. A politician changes his position on a critical issue to win over a big block of votes.

How would you describe yourself? Are you loyal to God and to those He has placed in your life? Do you defend those close to you when they are being wrongly accused? Will you put yourself on the line to stand by your church or your family?

In your quest for character, make loyalty a hallmark of your life.

Waging War on Pride

Charles Spurgeon said, "You cannot expect anything from God unless you put yourself in the right place, that is, as a beggar at his footstool. Then he will hear you, and not until then."

Important in building character is the realization of our own weaknesses. Although we try to mask our true feelings, we all struggle with the problem of pride. I once had a man tell me that he had no problem with pride. That was the one sin, he claimed, over which he had achieved victory. His boastful statement was evidence to the contrary.

Pride is a terrible demon to master. The minute we believe we are humble is the very minute our ego has crept onto center stage.

Why is pride so dangerous? It is dangerous because it is the precursor to greater sin. As soon as we think we are so far removed from temptation, we are vulnerable to falling. Pride convinces us to lower our guard. It gives us false confidence to flirt with sin, thinking we have the wherewithal to walk away.

I have seen many Christians over the years who fell into

sin, but they all admitted that it was a progression that started with pride. Sadly, every one of them would admit that they grew almost cocky. They thought that they were so spiritual they would be okay.

We must realize that our power is not in ourselves. It is in Christ. We don't have the capacity to keep ourselves from sin. We are weak and prone to its enslaving shackles. Only by living and walking in the strength of the Holy Spirit are we safe.

There is another type of pride that is dangerous as well. This is the pride of our spiritual ego. It is easy to get so caught up in the work of Christ, to win people to the Lord, to see great things happen and then step back and say, "Boy, am I wonderful." Now, no one would come out and say that, but we are often prone to think that. This is dangerous and must be done away with as soon as possible. Why? Because we'll start to justify little compromises, thinking God will overlook them because of our great service. Then, we'll head down the slippery slope of carnality.

Godly humility is not a sign of weakness, but a sign of real strength-strength in the power of God. Humility serves as a shield from sin, realizing how inadequate, how wretched we really are.

You'll never fully get a grip on humility until you get to Heaven, but you can ask the Lord to help you develop it now. By waging war on your pride, you'll add yet another crucial element to your foundation of character.

BEGIN CONSTRUCTION!

We've discussed at length the building materials that make up a foundation for a life of integrity, the only thing left is to begin construction. But, this is the hardest part.

There are three basic steps to help you get started in your journey towards integrity:

First, we must deal with our past. Take a long look at your past activities and confess any areas where you have been less than ethical. Ask the Lord's forgiveness and do what you can to make it right with the person or people you have wronged.

Second, we must commit ourselves to the principle of integrity. Now that you've cleared the past, commit yourself to each one of the principles we have discussed. Honesty, faithfulness, servanthood, loyalty, and humility are pillars of this new way of life. Find a spiritual mentor and make yourself accountable to him in these areas. List each of these virtues on a sheet of paper and write a periodic progress report. Check back in a few months to see how much you have grown and where you still need work.

Third, we must recognize the source of our strength. In your zeal for spiritual character, don't forget the source of your strength. On your own you will fail and fall back into a life of dishonesty. By walking in the Spirit, you will have the power to overcome temptation. (Galatians 5:24)

I encourage you to start construction right now, no matter where you are. Put the past aside, resolve to live better in the future, and ask the Lord for strength to discipline your spiritual life. Having built your foundation, you'll be ready when the storms of temptation come.

Take a moment to pray this prayer.

Thank you, Lord, for giving me Your Word. Help me to read it and pay attention to what it says. I pray that I will give the study of the Bible sufficient time in my busy schedule. Help me to put Your Word as top priority so I can continue to prepare the soil of my life for spiritual growth.

- TWO -

THE LURE OF TEMPTATION AND HOW TO RESIST IT

"And Pharaoh said unto his servants, Can we find such a one as this is, a man in whom the Spirit of God is?" (Genesis 41:38)

Temptation surrounds us on all sides. Billboards plaster images of men and women in suggestive poses. Television shows pride themselves on how raunchy and debased their characters act. Men and women in the workplace brag about their party lifestyles. The media gives a liberal slant on the issues while mocking old-fashioned values. Even the church is toning down its message to embrace a new tolerance. The Christian is bombarded on all sides with temptation.

Yet, we're told in 1 Corinthians 10:13 that temptation is nothing new: "There hath no temptation taken you but such as is common to man: but God is faithful, who will not suffer you to be tempted above that ye are able; but will with the temptation also make a way to escape, that ye may be able to bear it."

Since the serpent seduced Eve in the Garden of Eden, mankind has been encouraged to sin by the world, the flesh, and the devil. These three enemies of God have had one plan of action-to get us to ignore God's multitude of blessings and cause us to do the thing we know is wrong.

We must realize, however, that temptation in and of itself is not a sin. Jesus himself was tempted. (Hebrews 4:15) D. L. Moody echoed these thoughts: "When Christians find themselves exposed to temptation they should pray to God to uphold them, and when they are tempted they should not be discouraged. It is not a sin to be tempted; the sin is to fall into temptation."

The British playwright, Oscar Wilde said that the only thing he couldn't handle was temptation. In Scripture, however, we find the portrait of a man who found the spiritual strength to resist temptation. This man is Joseph and his story is found in Genesis 30-50.

Joseph was in a good news/bad news situation. Let me explain. The good news is that he was his father's favorite son. The bad news is that his jealous brothers sold him into slavery. The good news is that he wound up the chief of Potiphar's house, a prominent position. The bad news is Potiphar put Joseph in prison. The good news is that in jail, Joseph would meet two men who knew Pharaoh. The bad news is that upon release, one of these men died and the other would forget all about Joseph.

When he began his life, Joseph knew little about the twists and turns that would face him. Yet, we see that good breaks don't make a person of character and bad breaks don't break a person of character. Joseph was the example of one man who withstood the assaults of the world, the flesh, and the devil upon his character.

WEAPONS OF WARFARE

"And it came to pass after these things, that his master's wife cast her eyes upon Joseph; and she said, Lie with me. But he refused, and said unto his master's wife, Behold, my master wotteth not what is with me in the house, and he hath committed all that he hath to my hand; There is none greater in this house than I; neither hath he kept back any thing from me but thee, because thou art his wife: how then can I do this great wickedness, and sin against God?" (Genesis 39:7-9)

Three life principles armed Joseph against temptation and are good armor against temptation in today's world. First, we must fear God more than man. Resisting the advances of Potiphar's wife would bring certain ramifications. She was a manipulative woman with raw power in her grasp. How many other young men before Joseph had she cast into her net? None of these realities faced Joseph because he feared the wrath of God more than the wrath of the wicked.

Resisting temptation is not without its price, but the price of sin is much greater. The question to ask is not what will people think, but what will God think. That is the true test of character.

Therein lies the difference between image and character. Image asks, "What will happen if I get caught?" Character says, "What does God think of this activity?" Image thinks of earth-level implications, integrity thinks of spiritual consequences. Image is your perception in public, while integrity is your behavior in private.

Perhaps you are wary of becoming a dedicated believer because of the flak you will receive at work, in your family, or even at home. But, that persecution is nothing compared to the displeasure that compromise brings to the heart of God.

Integrity is why martyrs like Steven, John Hus, and William Tyndale could be tortured. They feared God more than they feared man. This principle guided their decision-making, even if it was life and death.

Secondly, we must know who we are in Christ. In the eyes of the world, Joseph was an unwanted slave, but in the eyes of God, he was a prized possession. He wasn't out to improve his lot or to raise his profile.

I've known many believers who are so concerned with what people perceive of them that they will make little compromises. An employee will backtalk the boss if it means getting in good with the power brokers at the company. A young girl will starve herself to get what she considers a perfect figure so she is accepted by her peers at school. A church may fudge their standards so they get bigger crowds on Sunday. A young mother may go into debt buying the fanciest clothes for her kids so the rich neighbors think highly of her.

Seeing ourselves in the sight of God helps us resist temptation because we will realize that we don't need anything this world has to offer to be successful. All we need is a relationship with God. Committing adultery with Potiphar's wife may have given Joseph an inside track to political power, but Joseph didn't need that. He didn't have an inferiority complex, instead he saw himself as God saw him and he was content in that.

The third weapon in our arsenal is the realization that men and women of character will be tempted. There are obstacles on the road to integrity. Joseph was clearly aware of these obstacles.

Some teach that once we trust Christ, there are no more trials, no more temptations, and no more hurdles to cross. Yet, Joseph's life says the opposite. He was a man bent on serving God, yet at every intersection, the devil was determined to take him down.

Peter gives us a sober warning against a cocky Christian attitude: "Be sober, be vigilant; because your adversary the devil, as a roaring lion, walketh about, seeking whom he may devour:" (1 Peter 5:8)

When we get puffed up and believe we are above being lured into sin, we are walking right into sin's painful trap. Our strength is not in our own power, but in the recognition of our weakness.

Let me put it to you frankly. The devil is pulling out all of the stops to ensure that you fall. Having lost the battle for your soul, he will try everything to make your life on this earth a complete loss for the Lord. Be wary of his cunning devices so you avoid becoming another sad statistic in the war against sin.

Nobody Will Know

"And it came to pass after these things, that his master's wife cast her eyes upon Joseph; and she said, Lie with me. But he refused, and said unto his master's wife, Behold, my master wotteth not what is with me in the house, and he hath committed all that he hath to my hand; There is none greater in this house than I; neither hath he kept back any thing from me but thee, because thou art his wife: how then can I do this great wickedness, and sin against God? And it came to pass, as she spake to Joseph day by day, that he hearkened not unto her, to lie by her, or to be with her. And it came to pass about this time, that Joseph went into the house to do his business; and there was none of the men of the house there within. And she caught him by his garment, saying, Lie with me: and he left his garment in her hand, and fled, and got him out." (Genesis 39:7-12)

Your family is on vacation; there is nobody at home but yourself. There it lies, the television remote. For once, you get to control what you watch. And the thoughts start creeping through your head. "Just this once, buddy, you won't get caught." "Nobody will ever know you watched it." "Just flip on that hot, new drama." "C'mon, live a little." And your fingers get weak. And your mind starts racing.

That's the first challenge to our integrity when we're tempted to sin. We think nobody will ever know. Joseph could have kept his adultery with Potiphar's wife a secret. Who would ever find out? The servants would be sworn to secrecy at the cost of their lives.

But, God would know and that was enough for Joseph. God is present when we're tempted as well. He knows what channels we flip to on the television. He knows the balances in our bank accounts. He knows the words we mutter at the driver who cuts us off. He knows the real truth behind politics in the office.

You may tell yourself that nobody knows, but that's a lie. A very dangerous lie. When we succumb to this falsehood, we begin working on image and abandon integrity. We start looking for cover, hiding so nobody finds out. Jesus warned that there is no way to hide sin:

"For there is nothing covered, that shall not be revealed; neither hid, that shall not be known. Therefore whatsoever ye have spoken in darkness shall be heard in the light; and that which ye have spoken in the ear in closets shall be proclaimed upon the housetops." (Luke 12:2-3)

Henry Hyde. Robert Livingston. Newt Gingrich. Bill Clinton. What do they have in common? They are all members of Congress who thought they hid their extramarital affairs. Nobody knew, except for a handful of close friends and aides. Yet, God knew. And when the spotlight was beamed onto their character, they were discovered and disgraced.

There are no corners or closets with God. He knows everything.

Just This Once

When I was a little kid, a graphic scene shook my consciousness. My father, a preacher in Kentucky, took me along on a visit to a family in the mountains. When we arrived, we discovered squalor. The inhabitants of the house were severe alcoholics. Under the messy bed was a dead baby. The parents were so drunk that they discovered the baby days after it had died.

These parents didn't set out to kill their baby. Yet, somewhere down the line, they bought the lie that there was no harm in one little sip of alcohol. "Just one, and I'll be done." Over the years one sip turned into several glasses which turned into a full-fledged addiction. At least one life could have been spared had they not taken the first sip.

Alexander MacClaren said, "The temptation once yielded to gains power. The crack in the embankment which lets a drop or two ooze through is soon a hole which lets out a flood."

Integrity is compromised, not all at once, but in a series of small steps. One harmless night of sex out of marriage can't be wrong, teens tell themselves. After all, everyone else is doing it. Before long, there is a pregnancy, a disappointed family, and a messed up life. One harmless click of a mouse onto a known pornographic site and we're down the road of sexual addiction. One little drag on a cigarette. Soon, the habit is increased to a pack a day, then a lifetime of smoking. Cancer sets in and we've reaped the terrible price.

It's a powerful lie we tell ourselves, Just one. We'll be okay. Then, we'll make everything right. Nobody's perfect. God will overlook everything.

Even when it is isolated to one occurrence, a compromise of integrity is painful enough. The shame, the looking-over-the-shoulder, the conviction of the Holy Spirit all bring suffering. Usually, we don't stop at one. We keep going further and further down the road of sin.

Joseph could have committed adultery once and gotten over it, but would that happen? He knew it wouldn't. She would want him more and more. He would become her pawn, her servant. More importantly, God would lose a witness in the Egyptian Kingdom.

Don't be fooled by the magic of the moment. That one-time journey into sin will lead to a lifetime of sorrow. Summoning the Spirit's strength to turn away at the beginning of sin will give you the protection against a lifetime of despair.

But, I'll Never Get Ahead!

"And Pharaoh said unto his servants, Can we find such a one as this is, a man in whom the Spirit of God is? And Pharaoh said unto Joseph, Forasmuch as God hath shewed thee all this, there is none so discreet and wise as thou art: Thou shalt be over my house, and according unto thy word shall all my people be ruled: only in the throne will I be greater than thou. And Pharaoh said unto Joseph, See, I have set thee over all the land of Egypt. And Pharaoh took off his ring from his hand, and put it upon Joseph's hand, and arrayed him in vestures of fine linen, and put a gold chain about his neck; And he made him to ride in the second chariot which he had; and they cried before him, Bow the knee: and he made him ruler over all the land of Egypt. And Pharaoh said unto Joseph, I am Pharaoh, and without thee shall no man lift up his hand or foot in all the land of Egypt." (Genesis 41:38-44)

He was a promising candidate. Like most politicians, we had a few questions about his position on critical issues, but we were sure that he believed much like we did. He promised us privately and publicly that on matters of morality, he would be strong.

We voted for him and elected him to office and were sorely disappointed. What was the very first bill that bore his signature? Sweeping legislation promoting the gambling industry. He sold out to the powerful lobby of the casino owners in the city. Another disappointment came on a critical pro-life bill. It passed with wide support in the General Assembly, but when it came to his desk, he vetoed it. His explanation? More calls came to his desk in support of abortion rights.

Compromise is no stranger to politics, to business, nor to other vocations where wheeling and dealing are considered necessary for survival. In fact, we're told that to get ahead, a person must rise above his values. Nice guys finish last, we've been told. Character is a high-ideal, but not politically feasible. Yet, the courage of Joseph reveals that integrity is not an enemy, but a catalyst of success. In fact, it was his very devotion to character that put him in the position of being chosen as Egypt's prime minister.

Contrary to worldly thinking, the risk of compromise isn't worth the reward of promotion. The pain of sin, whether it's broken marriage, damaged relationships, incarceration, or addiction isn't worth the pat on the back that comes with being the top dog at work, at home, or in politics.

The virtues of compromise are being extolled in many churches. As pastors, we're told that we must loosen up our standards, lighten up our preaching, and go to a more modern style to attract the audience. If we continue to preach the old-fashioned themes of Scripture, we'll never have big crowds.

This lie is predicated on a false view of success. It is God who judges our labors, not man. It is never right to do wrong to do right. When we rest our future in God's hands, He will take care of us. Like Joseph, rejecting temptation, even it means demotion, will result in promotion-by God.

I Deserve This

The cake was prepared, the hall was rented, and the guest list was double and triple-checked. It was going be a wonderful wedding. A Christian singer was set to marry a fellow singer. Everything was grand, except for one problem. They were newly divorced.

The singer recognized that God hates divorce, but after "ton's of marital counseling" she went to her pastors, loved ones, and ditched husband and told them, "I believe and trust that I've been released from this marriage." She explained her decision further. "I had an unshakeable, settling feeling about the path I was going to follow." What the singer's main counselor told her is the most disturbing. He said, "God made marriage for people. He didn't make people for marriage. He provided marriage so that people could enjoy each other to the fullest. I say if you have two people that are not thriving in a situation, I say remove the marriage." In other words, if your situation warrants it, do the wrong thing.

The Bible does give grounds for divorce in some occasions, and in those circumstances remarriage may be a good thing after a time of spiritual healing. However, the quick fleeing for greener pastures, like this gospel singer, was clearly a violation of God's sacred covenant. And her attitude-divorce because it feels good-is a telling sign of her motivation.

A very common lie we tell ourselves is, "I deserve it." My husband is not treating me right. My wife is not treating me right. I have been faithful my entire life. I deserve this little sin.

If anyone could use this defense it was Joseph. He could have said, "My brothers sold me into slavery. I've been left alone without family and friends. I deserve this." Surely, God wouldn't judge his adultery considering what he's been through. Right?

Wrong. God has so plainly spelled out his plan for our lives that we have no excuse to sin: "For this commandment which I command thee this day, it is not hidden from thee, neither is it far off. It is not in heaven, that thou shouldest say, Who shall go up for us to heaven, and bring it unto us, that we may hear it, and do it? Neither is it beyond the sea, that thou shouldest say, Who shall go over the sea for us, and bring it unto us, that we may hear it, and do it? But the word is very nigh unto thee, in thy mouth, and in thy heart, that thou mayest do it."

(Deuteronomy 30:11-13) That was God's instruction to Israel. Twentieth century Americans, who have the Bible in their grasp, who have freedom to worship, and who have been given so much scriptural light have little excuse.

We cannot use hardship as a reason to sin, because we have a great Friend in Christ who is there for our every need. (James 4:8) Trials are not justification for abandoning the godly life, but should motivate us to a greater holiness.

Your marriage may not be what you expected, but that is no excuse to give up on it. This is the time to discover scriptural methods to restoring vibrant love. Your childhood may have been dysfunctional, but God can heal your wounded heart and make you a man or woman of character. Your boss may mistreat you, but this is not an opportunity to undermine his authority, but a chance to show your Christ-like character.

We don't deserve to have a moment of sin. God deserves to have our very best.

But, I Can't Be a Joseph

As you reread the chronicle of Joseph's temptation, you may say to yourself, "But Joseph was different. He was a hero of the faith, so much stronger than me."

But, he wasn't. He had relationship problems. He had his share of bad breaks. He had disappointments. He had weaknesses. He had failures. He was human.

Let's revisit a verse we began with. I Corinthians tells us not only of the commonality of temptation, but also gives us the assurance that there is nothing in our lives that cannot be overcome with the help of the Holy Spirit:

"There hath no temptation taken you but such as is common to man: but God is faithful, who will not suffer you to be tempted above that ye are able; but will with the temptation also make a way to escape, that ye may be able to bear it." (1 Corinthians 10:13)

Joseph didn't resist temptation because of a great physical gift, but because of his focus on God. He fixed his eyes on the Creator. He drew his strength from the Lord, not from himself.

You can have the strength to resist temptation that Joseph possessed. Fix your eyes on the Creator. Wrap yourself in His arms and discover His Will for your life. Cultivate your walk with Him. Your love for Him will keep you from yielding when temptation knocks on your door. Like Joseph, the blessings of God will seem far more appealing to you than the lure of temptation.

- THREE -

THE PRICE OF A PAWN

For Herod himself had sent forth and laid hold upon John, and bound him in prison for Herodias' sake, his brother Philip's wife: for he had married her. For John had said unto Herod, It is not lawful for thee to have thy brother's wife. Therefore Herodias had a quarrel against him, and would have killed him; but she could not: For Herod feared John, knowing that he was a just man and an holy, and observed him; and when he heard him, he did many things, and heard him gladly. And when a convenient day was come, that Herod on his birthday made a supper to his lords, high captains, and chief estates of Galilee; And when the daughter of the said Herodias came in, and danced, and pleased Herod and them that sat with him, the king said unto the damsel, Ask of me whatsoever thou wilt, and I will give it thee. And he sware unto her, Whatsoever thou shalt ask of me, I will give it thee, unto the half of my kingdom. And she went forth, and said unto her mother, What shall I ask? And she said, The head of John the Baptist. And she came in straightway with haste unto the king, and asked, saying, I will that thou give me by and by in a charger the head of John the Baptist. And the king was exceeding sorry; yet for his oath's sake, and for their sakes which sat with him, he would not reject her. And immediately the king sent an executioner, and commanded his head to be brought: and he went and beheaded him in the prison, And brought his head in a charger, and gave it to the damsel: and the damsel gave it to her mother." (Mark 6:17-28)

Have you ever been the unwitting victim of someone else's agenda? Have you ever gotten deeply involved in a situation only to discover that you were being used? If so, you know what it is like to be a pawn. After you've discovered how your integrity was compromised, you are left with many regrets.

The gospel of Mark chronicles a sad tale of a young woman who allowed herself to be the pawn of another's wicked plot. The central characters are John the Baptist, Herod Antipas, Herod Philip, Herodias, and the pawn, Herodias' nameless daughter.

If this bizarre narrative were a soap opera, its appropriate title would be The Ugliness of Sin, but that wouldn't sell very well. Could you imagine the commercial? "And next, The Ugliness of Sin, followed by, As The World Turns."

John the Baptist was a man of courage and integrity who spoke the truth when it needed to be spoken. Herod Antipas was an admirer of John's ministry and according to Mark, "heard him gladly." Not that he listened. Herod didn't possess the character of John. Already married, he stole his brother, Herod Phillip's wife. Her name was Herodias and she engineered the marriage to ensure that she could be a full heir of Antipas' throne.

John knew this wasn't right and said so. He declared to Herod Antipas that he had no right to take his brother's wife. Herodias didn't particularly like this advice. John's words so enraged her that she privately wished him to be dead.

She got her wish. Herod held a birthday feast, but on the royal scale. The king invited all sorts of entertainment, including young women to dance before him and the other royalty in the kingdom. One of these was the young daughter of his new wife, Herodias. She danced before the king and pleased him so much that he offered her anything she desired, even half of the kingdom.

Her mother, Herodias, zoomed in on the scene. She whispered in her ear, "Ask for the head of John the Baptist!" So, this girl did. Regretfully, the drunken king had to follow through on his vow. He had John the Baptist killed and his head brought in on a platter.

As we look closely at this story, we can observe several important dynamics of character and the shining example of one man who refused to lower his convictions even at the cost of his life.

Just Say No!

"And he sware unto her, Whatsoever thou shalt ask of me, I will give it thee, unto the half of my kingdom. And she went forth, and said unto her mother, What shall I ask? And she said, The head of John the Baptist." Mark 6:23-24

How many times have you read the morning newspaper and scratched your head thinking, "How can someone do that?" Or perhaps you made a big mistake in your own life and you're left wondering, "How did I do this?"

It doesn't start out that way. Alcoholics don't begin with the desire to be a slave to alcohol. Adulterers don't intend to live a life of promiscuity. Those who embezzle money do not begin their career with the idea of cheating a company. Yet, it ends up that way.

Of all the things in the world, this young girl had no desire for the head of John the Baptist. Yet, she chose this over anything else in the kingdom. Why? She couldn't say no. She couldn't withstand the pressure.

We head down the road of destruction when we don't have the courage to say no. Somewhere down the line, a powerful personality, acceptance in a peer group, or a supposed friend convince us to fudge on our value system. For this woman, the powerful personality was her mother, Herodias. Charles Spurgeon said this: "Learn to say no; it will be of more use to you than to be able to speak Latin."

This girl had no self-worth. She lived off the opinions of others. She danced to the delight of the Herodian men, selling her body for their pleasure. Her sense of purpose came only from satisfying the base appetites of those around her.

It is easy to get our sense of self-worth from the wrong places. Hollywood tells us that sex appeal is everything. Madison Avenue convinces us that we have to have the right clothing. Our peer groups tells us that "everybody" is doing it. Even our family may smirk at our old-fashioned ways.

Like this girl, we are fooled into believing that others' opinions are the benchmark of success. We do whatever it takes to garner that praise.

The problem with such thinking is that society's values shift. According to a recent Gallup poll, 52% of Americans no longer believe premarital sex is wrong. In 1969, only 21% of Americans held that opinion. Lifestyles we would shudder at years ago are now in the mainstream.

If we build our lives on these shifting values, our foundations will erode when the storms of pressure come. The pressures will be strong. We will face pressure from family to compromise our Christian beliefs. We'll face pressure from the employer to be less than honest with clients. We will face pressure from colleagues to give less than our best to our family and our ministry.

We can only resist peer pressure by building our lives on a solid foundation, Jesus Christ. This young girl's whole life was wrapped up in others' opinions of her and thus in the moment of decision, she made a terrible mistake. If we fail to anchor our security in Jesus Christ, we will also make terrible mistakes.

The Apostle Paul counseled the Philippian believers, who lived in an ungodly environment to find their confidence, not in the opinions of men, but in their position in Christ. "Therefore, my brethren dearly beloved and longed for, my joy and crown, so stand fast in the Lord, my dearly beloved." (Philippians 4:1)

As you struggle with tough issues in your life, make Paul's admonition a motto for your own life. Know that the world's opinion is unimportant. You don't have to relent to the tremendous pressures around you. You can say no, because you are pleasing God, whose evaluation is the only evaluation that matters.

A Root of Bitterness

"And she came in straightway with haste unto the king, and asked, saying, I will that thou give me by and by in a charger the head of John the Baptist." Mark 6:25

Jenny was beginning a new career. She saw an ad in the paper for a telemarketing position, so she sent a resume. The company hired her. On her first day, she was given a little cubicle and a list of names. The boss told her to go at it. Lacking experience both in sales and in telephone skills, she bungled the first call. When she hung up, her co-workers burst out laughing and her boss shouted above the roar, "This is the worst telemarketer I have ever heard!"

Jenny put on a good front, but privately she seethed. How was she supposed to know how to sell things over the phone? This was her first day! From that day on, she swore she would get even. She would never be embarrassed like that again. Over the next few months, she bought every book on sales and marketing. She went to conferences and consulted experts. Slowly, Jenny began to be successful. After a year, she became the top sales person in her company. At the annual party, she was awarded top salesman. But, her anger over that first day's humiliation never left. When asked to speak to the group, she didn't acknowledge the award. She didn't thank her superiors. She simply said two words, "I quit," and walked off the stage, never to work for that company again.

Jenny, too, was a pawn, but rather than being enslaved to another's expectations, she was a prisoner of her bitterness. She allowed one slight to fester inside of her and guide her thinking. As a result, she gave up a promising career.

Herodias never dealt with her bitterness either. She was angry at John the Baptist for speaking out against her adultery. Caught red-handed, she sought to make this disciple suffer by manipulating those around her. She would have her way and nobody would stop her.

The Bible declares revenge to be the Lord's job, not ours. Often our anger, like Herodias' is unjustified and it is our response to the conviction of the Holy Spirit regarding a sin. Rather than dealing with our heart, we lash out at the messenger.

Other times, we have reason to be offended. Like Jenny, we may have been wronged, slighted, or humiliated. This tiny bitterness, when left unchecked, grows and grows until revenge becomes an obsession. We're warned against this in Hebrews: "Looking diligently lest any man fail of the grace of God; lest any root of bitterness springing up trouble you, and thereby many be defiled;" (Hebrews 12:15)

The danger of bitterness is that it is blinding. We get so caught up in our own rage, that we cannot see God's purpose in allowing the circumstance. Our obsession to get even leads us to engage in activity we know to be wrong.

This type of behavior is destructive because it pulls other people into our web. And in our desire to get even, we injure innocent people. Jenny's company suffered a significant loss with her absence. What about the other sales staff who had to pick up the slack. They would have to work longer hours until a new salesman took her place. This would take them away from their families.

Herodias employed many people in her plot. She manipulated her husband into imprisoning John the Baptist. She used her daughter to ask for the head of John the Baptist. She put unnecessary pressure on other people to do things that were wrong.

When we become full of our own bitterness, we put pressure on others to compromise their integrity. We manipulate others to help us in our attempt to get even.

We may never chop off a disciple's head, but our attempts to push our program can cause serious injury to the Body of Christ. We destroy meaningful relationships. We get others in trouble by asking them to do things that are not right. We create an atmosphere of dishonesty.

Perhaps you have resentment in your heart toward a person or a group. Maybe you are angry with the position of your church. You'll be tempted to start a faction of disgruntled members. Perhaps you've been wronged at work. You'll be tempted to work behind the scenes to put pressure on your boss. You may have a conflict with a close friend. You'll be tempted to talk behind his back with other friends.

If you are angry because you've been caught, confess your sin to God and ask for His forgiveness. If your bitterness is because of a wrong, forgive as God has forgiven you. The Bible says that revenge is of the Lord. (Romans 12:19) Above all, never seek revenge, because that will blind you to what God has in store for your life.

WHO CARES?

"And immediately the king sent an executioner, and commanded his head to be brought: and he went and beheaded him in the prison, And brought his head in a charger, and gave it to the damsel: and the damsel gave it to her mother." (Mark 6:27-28)

A recent news article described how dozens of tourists watched impassively as a woman drowned while trying to save her child. One person even videotaped the drowning, saying "I got the whole thing on tape." No one watching made any attempt to help.

There were no video cameras in the days of John the Baptist, but there were many spectators who stood by as an innocent man was killed. They enjoyed his preaching, admired his courage, and undoubtedly mourned his loss. Yet every one of them looked the other way when this act was carried out. Their cowardice prevented them from standing up for the one who, according to Jesus was "the greatest man who ever lived."

A worse condition than outright wickedness is a state of spiritual apathy. Jesus said that He would rather we be hot (spiritually on-fire) or cold (spiritually frozen) than lukewarm. (Revelation 3:13-16).

Here are some major dangers of apathy:

Apathy keeps us from sharing our faith. Amy Carmichael

once had a powerful dream. She dreamt that people were falling off a cliff while nearby another group of people were busy constructing daisy chains. They knew the danger nearby, but were more preoccupied with their important "projects." As believers, we become so preoccupied with career, family, and job that we ignore the hurting masses around us. Apathy keeps us from fulfilling the Great Commission.

Apathy allows little issues to become large problems. When we fail to deal with little problem areas of our life, they grow and soon become unmanageable. A problem of lust can escalate into a crisis point in marriage. Poor money management can lead to bankruptcy and ruin. Slight rebellion can turn a child into a prodigal if not addressed.

Apathy hurts the needy. That neighbor who struggles to put food on the table. The little boy whose parents are in a custody battle. The relative who is asking spiritual questions. We may be the only person who can help them. When we brush them off, their needs go unmet. An unsaved person may never again hear the Gospel. A child may never have the chance at a good influence. A seeking relative may fall prey to a cult. All because we didn't care enough to get involved.

Apathy hurts the heart of God. God cared enough to send His Son; do we care enough to stand up for what is right? When we don't care enough to do the right thing, even in the face of danger, we are making a bold statement that Christ doesn't mean enough. He's worth a lot, but not enough to risk losing something valuable.

It is easy to rationalize our non-action. We miss a church activity to rest. We ignore that hurting co-worker because of our own problems. We ignore warning signs in our children's behavior because they are "just kids." We don't say anything about unethical practices at work, because that is the "real world."

How do we fight apathy? By looking at life through spiritual eyes. See the real battle, between right and wrong. Understand the plan of the adversary, Satan. It is his desire to take you from God's will and render your life unfit for service. He'll try any means, and his greatest means is to make you comfortable enough to ignore what is really important.

CHECKMATE

As you examine the bizarre tale in Mark 6, you'll begin to see who the real hero is: John the Baptist. We can learn how to be a man or woman of character by looking not at those who lived, but at the courageous disciple who died.

The impact of Herod, Herodias, and the royal family has long evaporated, but the legacy of John the Baptist's testimony lives on. He was a real man of integrity.

John refused to endorse a lifestyle he knew to be wrong in the sham marriage of Herod Antipas and his brother, Phillip's wife, Herodias. John spoke up, even though he knew it would cost him. No amount of money could buy his silence.

We do not see signs of bitterness in him after being imprisoned. We read of no escape attempts or political maneuvering to strike back at Herodias. He clearly left the revenge up to the Lord.

And apathy was not even in John's vocabulary. He couldn't sit by while sin was taking place in the palace. He clearly communicated God's disdain for Herod's adulterous lifestyle.

John exemplified character by his testimony and is an inspiration for every Christian. In Matthew 11, Jesus said of John: " . . . Among them that are born of women there hath not risen a greater than John the Baptist . . ."

Yet, the last part of Jesus' assessment of John gives hope to even the weakest Christian, "notwithstanding he that is least in the kingdom of heaven is greater than he." You and I have a greater ability to emulate the character of John because we have the Holy Spirit living inside of us.

Perhaps you have failed the test of character in your life. Maybe you've been a pawn to ungodly activity. You have stood by and watched while others engaged in sin. Take heart and know that God can take you where you are and shape you into a man or woman of character.

- FOUR -

IF IT FEELS GOOD DON'T DO IT!

For 500 years, a gigantic tree stood in a Colorado forest, enduring wind, hail storms, and even an earthquake. It was a tiny sapling when Columbus landed in San Salvador, a "young" 284 years old when the Declaration of Independence was signed, and "middle-aged" during the Civil War. However, it just recently fell to the ground. The cause? It wasn't a violent storm or the work of loggers. No, the persistent gnawing of tiny beetles tore away at the inner fibers. After 500 years of infiltration, the tree was finally unable to hold up its own weight.

The character of a Christian, like that tree, is torn, not by large objects, but the incessant gnawing of the sins of the flesh. Like the tiny beetle, sin creeps ever-so-slowly into the fiber of our lives with a destructive purpose in mind. Unless we deal with this infiltration, eventually we too will fall.

Typically, it is one particular "species" of sin that tears away at our spiritual growth. Some call this the besetting sin. I call it the Mr. or Mrs. Sin: it's the one sin that we grapple with most. In Hebrews 12:1, we're encouraged to lay it aside if we desire to successfully run the race: "Wherefore seeing we also are compassed about with so great a cloud of witnesses, let us lay aside every weight, and the sin which doth so easily beset us, and let us run with patience the race that is set before us"

For some, the Mr. or Mrs. Sin is a problem with lust. For others it is a lack of faith that leads to constant worry. Some struggle with pride-overconfidence in self and belittling the contributions of others. Then, there are those whose problem area is laziness.

While the type of Mr. or Mrs. Sin may vary from person to person-the nature of it is the same. It is the sin that tempts us the most and needs the most discipline to overcome. It is also the sin that will make or break our progress in the Christian life.

In the Old Testament, we're given an example of a man who failed to overcome his Mr. Sin. Unlike Joseph, whose godly character shone in a moment of temptation, Samson failed nearly every spiritual test.

Rejecting the Norm

Born of godly parents, Samson was put in a position to succeed. In Judges 13, we're given a brief biography of his parents. They were God-fearing, yet had not been blessed with children until Samson was miraculously sent by God.

Samson had a special designation and special purpose. He was to take the vow of a Nazarite which had three important disciplines: 1) He was not to consume anything from the vine. 2) He was not to touch anything dead. And 3) He was not to cut his hair.

These are unusual requirements, but Samson was an unusual man. God set him aside to be a judge over Israel. He was to stand out among his people as a man of holiness and dependence upon God. The typical Nazarite vow lasted for a short time, but Samson was different. His vow was to last a lifetime.

Tragically, Samson rejected his heritage. He grew up to despise everything God had given him, including his parents and his special designation by God. He not only violated his Nazarite vow by a) drinking wine, b) touching a dead lion carcass, and c) cutting his hair, but also he violated God's law by marrying a Philistine woman.

By his very nature, Samson was a rebel. Unhappy within the borders of Israel and the confines of his heritage, he ventured into enemy (Philistine) territory and into a life of sin.

Like Samson, we all have temptation to rebel when things don't go the way we envision. A teen bristles at the "rules" imposed by parents. A spouse is unhappy with his or her mate. An employee is annoyed by the personality of his boss. A church member is uncomfortable with the high standards of a church.

Popular teaching suggests that rebellion is a good thing-even to be applauded. We're told that right and wrong are relative and that the only moral barometer is what makes us feel good. Yet, we see in Scripture that breaking from the norm-God's standard of righteousness-is no virtue. "For rebellion is as the sin of witchcraft, and stubbornness is as iniquity and idolatry." 1 Samuel 15:23

Samson was so preoccupied with getting what he wanted, by fulfilling his desires, that he missed God's special call on his life. He wasted a chance to become a spiritual leader in Israel and an agent of change in an era of godlessness.

We also are in danger of missing God's best when we give in to what we want. As the body of Christ, we have been set aside for a special purpose. "But ye are a chosen generation, a royal priesthood, an holy nation, a peculiar people; that ye should shew forth the praises of him who hath called you out of darkness into his marvellous light" 1 Peter 2:9

God's desire is that His children become agents of change in the world. Our special mission is to share the light of God's love with a lost and dying world. Yet, we endanger that mission when we give in to the desires of the flesh.

DEFINING FUN

For Samson, the holy life seemed too stuffy and confining. He was a fun-loving guy. He bought the lie that enjoyment comes only when we break the rules. "That's what rules are for, right?" I could almost hear him saying.

The world has cleverly deceived people into believing that to have a good time, we must break the rules. Yet, that is not the case. According to a national study, one in four college students are classified as binge drinkers and nearly one in four admit to binging once a week. At Penn State, about 200 binge drinkers end up in the emergency room every year. The campus police report that in the year 2000, there were 300 alcohol related arrests. We're told that unless you drink you are not "cool" and you don't know how to "have a good time." But, I ask, is throwing up in the sink, getting arrested for violent behavior, or even injuring someone on the road "a good time?" Momentary pleasure has its consequences. Relationships are damaged. Reputations are destroyed. Children are affected. The downward spiral continues.

Blinded by the pleasure of the moment, Samson couldn't see the far-reaching effects of his actions. He didn't measure the long-term consequences: losing his eyesight, languishing in a Philistine prison, then dying. His was a gifted life wasted. All he saw was the here and now.

God had a much better way for Samson, and he has a much better way for you and me. God focuses on the internal, rather than the external and thus grants a life of long-lasting peace and satisfaction. In the end, we experience true joy that comes from living within the borders of His Will.

It is a lie that says you have to sin to be happy. The years since I have trusted Christ have been much more fun than my years in the world. If you could peak into our living room on a given night, you'd agree. You would probably find us laughing and enjoying each others' company and yet we haven't had a sip of alcohol, rented a questionable movie, or sought any other form of recreation that brings dishonor to Christ's name.

Believe it or not, happiness and holiness can coexist. A.W. Tozer says this: "One may easily deceive himself by cultivating a religious joy without a corresponding righteous life. No man should desire to be happy who is not at the same time holy. He should spend his efforts in seeking to know and do the will of God, leaving to Christ the matter of how happy he shall be ."

True joy is found only when we focus our energy on fulfilling God's Will. The benefits are incomparable. We have peace because we can entrust our future to an all-wise, all-caring God. We escape the problems that accompany a miserable life of sin. We have the satisfaction of knowing that we are contributing to the family of God.

THROWING AWAY GOD'S BEST

It was one of the saddest days of my life. I had to do the funeral of a young Christian who grew up in our church. After high-school, he strayed from his Christian roots, getting involved in the party lifestyle. He fathered a child out of wedlock. Time after time, we tried to reach out to him, but he never heeded our warnings. Finally, God had enough and took his life. Full of drugs, he wandered onto a busy freeway near his house and was struck by a car. When we got the news, we were saddened. The mother grieved, and we all wondered what could have happened had he served the Lord.

It's never too late to begin again, but sometimes we use that as an excuse to continue in a sinful lifestyle. Like Samson, we tell ourselves, "Someday, I'll get it right." Meanwhile, years that could have been productive go down the drain and we toss away a life that could have been used by God. We test the grace of God. Romans 6:1 asks, *"What shall we say then? Shall we continue in sin, that grace may abound?"* The answer, in the next verse, is a resounding, "God forbid."

God is gracious, but He is also just and will punish sin. That is a bedrock truth. Paul warns in Galatians: "Be not deceived; God is not mocked: for whatsoever a man soweth, that shall he also reap. For he that soweth to his flesh shall of the flesh reap corruption; but he that soweth to the Spirit shall of the Spirit reap life everlasting." (Galatians 6:7-8)

After repeated warnings, God will eventually put us "on the shelf" (John 15:2) where we are out of His protective will and are not of any use to the Kingdom of Christ. We are still assured of Heaven (John 10:28), but we are no longer fit for service. This was Paul's greatest fear and should be the greatest fear of every Christian. (1 Corinthians 9:27) If our sin is great enough, He may even take us home.

Your flesh will tell you that character is meaningless and that there are no consequences for sin. For a while, it will seem as though you are getting away with it. You may even think God is blessing you. Yet, as we have learned through the life of Samson and others who have strayed off God's path, sin has its price. The risk is definitely not worth the reward.

REPLACEMENT: GOD'S HOW TO MANUAL

When I counsel people who have a problem controlling their sin, the most common plea I hear is, "I know it's wrong-but I can't help it." For Samson, the desires of his flesh had such a strong pull that it seemed impossible to overcome.

Yet, God gave us a prescription for success. Many times we think that the answer is to simply stop the activity and then we'll be spiritually "okay." That's not the answer. Those desires, those rages within us must be filled with something else. Ephesians 5:18 says *"And be not drunk with wine, wherein is excess; but be filled with the Spirit;"*

The answer is to begin walking in the spirit. That is how the Mr. or Mrs. Sin is eradicated. We'll never achieve perfection on this earth, but we can build up our spiritual immune system. We definitely don't have to be a slave to our flesh.

We can have victory over sin because Jesus Christ has power over it. 2000 years ago, sin was defeated on the cross of Calvary. That same power exists inside of each believer in the person of the Holy Spirit. When we walk in that Spirit, we are assured that we will not give in to the desires of our flesh. (Galatians 5:16)

Perhaps you're discouraged because you have given in to your flesh. Maybe Mr. or Mrs. Sin has ruled your life. I'd like to tell you that you can begin anew. You can start fresh. It is never too late to start over. Even Samson's life became a glory to God at the very end. In Hebrews 11, he is mentioned with the prophets.

    I don't know where you are. You may look back and see many wasted years away from the Lord. If this is so, let me encourage you to start where you are.

    You may be a new Christian. Let me encourage you to have a watchful eye for sin. This is the time to build up your defenses and begin your walk with God on the right foot.

    I'm guessing that you are somewhere in between. You may not be rebellious like Samson, yet you are aware of sins in your life that have been ignored. You know these sins should be addressed. Today I challenge you to begin the purging process.

    Whatever stage you are at, be assured that you are not fighting sin alone. The Holy Spirit is ever-present and ready to help you overcome the desires of the flesh and live victoriously. With His power, you'll see your life changed in a dramatic way.

- FIVE -

STANDING WATCH
PRACTICAL PRINCIPLES
FOR PROTECTING YOUR PURITY

"Abram dwelled in the land of Canaan, and Lot dwelled in the cities of the plain, and pitched his tent toward Sodom." (Genesis 13:12)

In best-selling book, *Fast-Food Nation,* Eric Schlosser describes a secret, military installation:

> Cheyenne Mountain sits on the eastern slope of Colorado's Front Range, rising steeply from the prairie and overlooking the city of Colorado Springs. From a distance, the mountain appears beautiful and serene, dotted with rocky outcroppings, scrub oak, and ponderosa pine. It looks like the backdrop of an old Hollywood western, just another gorgeous Rocky Mountain vista. And yet Cheyenne Mountain is hardly pristine. One of the nation's most important military installations lies deep within it, housing units of the North American Aerospace Command, the Air Force Space Command, and the United States Space Command. During the mid-1950s, high-level officials at the Pentagon worried that America's air defenses had become vulnerable to sabotage and attack. Cheyenne Mountain was chosen as the site for a top-secret, underground combat operations center. The mountain was hollowed out, and fifteen buildings, most of them three

stories high, were erected amid a maze of tunnels and passageways extending for miles. The four-and-a-half-acre underground complex was designed to survive a direct hit by an atomic bomb. Now officially called the Cheyenne Mountain Air Force Station, the facility is entered through steel blast doors that are three feet thick and weigh twenty-five tons each; they automatically swing shut in less than twenty seconds. The base is closed to the public, and a heavily armed quick response team guards against intruders. Pressurized air within the complex prevents contamination by radioactive fallout and biological weapons. The buildings are mounted on gigantic steel springs to ride out an earthquake or the blast wave of a thermonuclear strike. The hallways and staircases are painted slate gray, the ceilings are low, and there are combination locks on many of the doors. A narrow escape tunnel, entered through a metal hatch, twists and turns its way out of the mountain through solid rock. Fifteen hundred people work inside the mountain, maintaining the facility and collecting information from a worldwide network of radars, spy satellites, ground-based sensors, airplanes, and blimps. The Cheyenne Mountain Operations Center tracks every manmade object that enters North American airspace or that orbits the earth. It is the heart of the nation's early warning system. It can detect the firing of a long-range missile, anywhere in the world, before that missile has left the launch pad.

The Cheyenne Mountain Air Force Station has one purpose: to protect the interests of the United States by monitoring everything that enters its borders. The successful Christian also sets up a warning system in the borders of his life, carefully analyzing what he allows in and out of his life.

It is easy to get puffed up and believe that we are strong enough not to fall into sin. We might hear of the struggles of a fellow believer and we proudly dismiss him as weak, yet ignore our own frailty. We know from Scripture that the power to resist evil and do right is not a power of our own, but a dependency upon the Holy Spirit's strength.

We are all sinners by nature and even the greatest Christians have the capacity to do evil. The Apostle Paul warned the believers in Corinth against this self-righteousness:

"Wherefore let him that thinketh he standeth take heed lest he fall." (1 Corinthians 10:12)

Rather than rely on a perceived strength, we should seek to build our spiritual defenses. When we acknowledge our weakness and our dependence upon Christ, we'll do everything we can to protect our spiritual purity and prevent sin from creeping into our borders.

I've often been asked, "Why do so many people fall into sin?" My answer is usually that these people were not prepared for temptation. They falsely believed that they were immune to great moral lapses and therefore opened themselves up to the gradual wooing of the flesh.

Lot was a great example. As a Christian, he saw the beautifully watered plains of Jordan and began to settle his family there. This piece of land was facing the wicked city of Sodom. I can hear the thoughts going back and forth in Lot's head. *It's not all that bad. I can handle it. I wouldn't ever live like that. I'm so strong, I can resist those temptations.* Yet, the end of Lot's life is tragic. God had to rescue him from Sodom and Gomorrah before it was destroyed. He later committed incest with his daughters. At the beginning of his life, Lot didn't intend to become a citizen of Sodom, but he refused to eliminate the surrounding temptations. He didn't put up his spiritual defenses and was thus left vulnerable to sin's attack.

As believers, we often pitch our tent toward Sodom as did Lot, foolishly believing we are strong enough to resist its lure. We tell ourselves that God will keep us from evil. We may even pray that. Why do we test our weakness? Why do we court sin so openly?

Our purity is compromised not all at once, but in a series of slow processes, mainly because we have lowered our guard and have not kept a watchful eye on what we allow to enter our lives and influence our heart.

We can avoid a life of trouble by establishing a set of standards-a code of conduct. By living within the safe haven, we can protect what is most important to us: our personal purity. By establishing and following guidelines, we protect ourselves from sin's attack. Here are some practical tips on guarding your purity:

Have an answer before the question. That sounds backward, but actually it is backward to wait for the question before we are ready to answer. In Daniel 1, we read how this young Israelite already had a plan before he got to the King's palace. Verse 8 says he "purposed in his heart" that he would not violate the Mosaic law. There were thousands of young Jewish boys taken into captivity, yet Daniel and his three friends seem to be the only ones who were strong enough to take a stand. Why? Because they established beforehand that they would not disobey God.

Many times, we can avoid the so-called "gray" areas of Christian living by committing ourselves to God before we are faced with tough decisions. Families should set a standard for TV viewing before flipping on the tube. Employees should promise not to bend the office rules before they are approached with a temptation. Young people should set the ground rules for dating before they begin a relationship. By knowing the answer first, we can do a much better job of answering the unavoidable tough questions.

Avoid the appearance of evil. Our church staff has a rigid policy which others may call extreme. However, we have avoided many problems this way. We don't allow married men or women to travel with other married men or women alone in a car. Why? Why even take such a risk?

In counseling, we also encourage men to counsel men and women to counsel women. In the rare exception where a man has to counsel a woman, that man must have his wife present. Why is this important? Because we care not only about our inner character, but also about our reputation.

Much evil can be avoided by avoiding the appearance of evil. If a colleague of the opposite sex asks you out to lunch, take other people with you and don't ride alone in the car. They may think you are crazy, but a little mocking is better than the threat to your integrity. Remember you don't know your own weaknesses. Don't put yourself in a tempting situation that you may or may not have the power to resist. It is better to avoid the opportunity for sin altogether.

Desperate times take desperate measures. We shouldn't do anything to facilitate our weaknesses, which differ from person to person. We should take extreme measures to get rid of the object of our temptation. Obviously, we can't be isolated from the world, but we can remove things that have the power to hurt us spiritually. I know one young man who had a terrible longing to listen to the wrong types of music, so he literally ripped the radio out of his car. I don't expect everyone to have to do that, but I do admire the man for dealing with his problem. Some families should consider getting rid of their television if it is becoming a negative influence. Others should cancel their internet subscription if the vast amount of pornography presents a struggle too hard to bear. The Holy Spirit has promised to help us fight sin, but He also expects us to do our part in resisting it.

Stay active for God. King David's adultery with Bathsheba could have been avoided-if only David was where he was supposed to be-in battle with his men. But, when everyone was away, he had idle time and he not only committed adultery, but also murdered a man. An old proverb says that idle hands are the devil's workshop. Many of those wasted hours on television could be spent profitably somewhere else, helping at church, volunteering at a homeless shelter, or spending time with a shut-in. Late nights cruising the Internet may be spent catching up on sleep or reading a book. We get into trouble when we have too much unregulated, unsupervised time on our hands. That's when the Devil begins tempting us.

Of the Christians I have seen fall, the majority stopped being active. They gradually began missing church until they stopped going altogether. They shared later that they stopped doing their devotions on a daily basis. Just like our physical bodies need to be regularly fed and exercised, our spiritual bodies need that same maintenance, otherwise we quickly grow out of shape and are prone to injury. Keep a regular pattern of church attendance, Bible reading, prayer, and witnessing and you will have less time to wander into tempting activities

Chose godly aquaintances. Whether we admit it or not, we are influenced by the company we keep. There are many things we wouldn't do on our own, but pressured by the crowd, we give in. Find and keep good friendships in the church. Fellowship with people who have the same values and who will influence you to follow God. You may be forced to cut off long-time friendships with unsaved or carnal friends, but if you are serious about keeping your character, you will come to see that your Christian friends are much more valuable.

True friends make you accountable to God. They will lovingly steer you back onto the right path when you wander. They will help you see through doubts and fears of your faith and will not let you walk into compromising situations.

Undergo a periodic checkup. The yearly checkup. We hate them, yet as we get older, we know that they are necessary if we want to keep living healthy. Spiritual checkups are important too. Every so often, we need to renew our dedication to the Lord and to His pattern for our lives. It doesn't have to be a public statement. It can be a private affirmation.

A convicting sermon, a powerful book, a tragic circumstance, or even a quiet time in the Word can all present moments of reflection and deep soul-searching. In the rush of the everyday, we are tempted to ignore these subtle promptings of the Holy Spirit. Yet these are moments that shape our character. They alert us to an area of weakness and call us to a greater commitment to Christ.

Periodic checkups keep us from straying too far off the path God has called us to walk.

Avoid snap decisions. Sometimes what seems right at the moment is really the wrong course of action. Never make a major decision without spending time to think about it. How will it affect your service to the Lord? What are the implications upon your family? What is your motive for making the decision? Ask yourself these questions and more before proceeding.

After careful prayer, seek godly counsel. Always get the advice of a pastor or lay leader in your church. They can step back and give an unbiased opinion. They are not emotionally involved and therefore can render a spiritually mature verdict. Even though I am a senior pastor, I get counsel for every major decision I make. I have men whom I consider my spiritual leaders with whom I talk things over. Then, I usually seek the advice of someone knowledgeable in the field. If I'm buying a car, I seek the advice of a trusted mechanic. If I'm purchasing a new home, I have tradesmen do a walk-through. If the church is considering a partnership, I talk to people who have dealt with that particular organization in the past.

Before we do anything significant, we must do our homework. This not only prevents us from wasting time and money, but it also keeps us from getting involved in something that could damage our reputation or character.

QUEST FOR CHARACTER

Your character is everything. Don't take this responsibility lightly. Like Daniel and Joseph, be ready when the storms of temptation come.

The Lord desires that you become a man or woman of character-a light in this dark world. There are people in your world who are watching you, investigating your faith to see if it is real or just a passing fad. They want to see a changed life before they put their faith in the Christ you profess.

Perhaps you have ignored your character. The good news is that you can start right now-right where you are. Put aside your past by confessing it to God. Then, begin living for Him anew.

Though the world says that your personal integrity is not important, God says it is. I encourage you to begin the journey towards integrity today.

Notes

Chapter Three
1. "Tourists Watched Woman Drown," *The Courier-Journal*, Louisville, Kentucky, 29 August 1994, A3.

Chapter Four
1. "Smashed: Kids and Alcohol", msnbc.com, July 14th, 200.1
2. A.W. Tozer, *The Price of Neglect* (Christian Publications) p. 3-309, quoted from Marilyn E. Foster, *Tozer on the Holy Spirit*, (Camp Hill, PA: Christian Publications, 2000), July 16th entry.

Chapter Five
1. Adapted from the Introduction to *Fast Food Nation*, by Eric Schlosser (New York: Houghton Mifflin Company, 2001).

How to Know for Sure You are Going to Heaven

- Realize first, that everyone is less perfect than a holy God. We are all sinners and unable to save ourselves.
  For all have sinned, and come short of the glory of God; Romans 3:23

- God says that even our good deeds are unclean in His sight. Our good deeds can never pay the price for our sin.
  But we are all as an unclean thing, and all our righteousnesses are as filthy rags; and we all do fade as a leaf; and our iniquities, like the wind, have taken us away. Isaiah 64:6

- The result and penalty of sin is death, which means separation from God forever.
  For the wages of sin is death; but the gift of God is eternal life through Jesus Christ our Lord. Romans 6:23

- Because we have sinned, we all deserve to be separated from God forever. God hates sin because it separates us from Him but He loves us, the sinner.

- Heaven is a perfect place; therefore no sin can enter there. Man must be perfect to gain entrance.
  And there shall in no wise enter into it any thing that defileth, neither whatsoever worketh abomination, or maketh a lie: but they which are written in the Lamb's book of life. Rev. 21:27

- Nothing man can do could help obtain the perfection God requires for Heaven.
  For by grace are ye saved through faith; and that not of yourselves: it is the gift of God: Not of works, lest any man should boast. Ephes. 2:8-9

- Salvation is only by God's grace. Grace means unmerited favor or undeserved mercy. A gift is not earned or paid for or it would not be a gift.
  But to him that worketh not, but believeth on him that justifieth the ungodly, his faith is counted for righteousness. Romans 4:5

- Christ made a complete payment for all sin and offers His righteousness to us.
  For he hath made him to be sin for us, who knew no sin; that we might be made the righteousness of God in him. 2 Cor. 5:21

- We have seen that we are all sinners and that the penalty of sin is eternal separation from God. We have also seen that God loves us and offers us the gift of eternal life. He requires only our belief, our trust in that payment.

- How could a holy God give eternal life to sinners? Only through His Son who died on the cross to make a full payment for all sin.

- All we have to do to have eternal life is believe in Jesus Christ.
  For God so loved the world, that he gave his only begotten Son, that whosoever believeth in him should not perish, but have everlasting life. John 3:16

This verse does not say anything about promising God good works in order to be saved. It doesn't mention joining a church or being baptized or even quitting all your sinning. The word *believe* means to trust, depend, or rely upon.

- Will you place your trust in Jesus Christ to save your soul? To trust Him means to rely totally on Him, not on your own good works. Will you do this right now?

- If you have trusted Jesus Christ as your Savior, then you can know you have eternal life. God has promised this in His Word.

    These things have I written unto you that believe on the name of the Son of God; that ye may <u>know</u> that ye have eternal life, and that ye may believe on the name of the Son of God. 1 John 5:13

MORE GREAT BOOKLETS IN DR. SCUDDER'S CHRISTIAN LIVING SERIES

- *THE ART OF MARRIAGE*
- *YOUR MONEY, GOD'S WISDOM*
- *FOREVER WITH GOD?*
- *THE LORD IS MY SHEPHERD*
- *THE END OF TIME*
- *MORE THAN A MIRACLE*

Quentin Road Ministries
60 Quentin Road • Lake Zurich, IL 60047
1800-78-GRACE • www.qrm.org